KB265090

The Flying Trunk

Little Storyteller
The Flying Trunk 하늘을 나는 가방

저자 Chalice Kerr

초판 1쇄 인쇄 2012년 3월 5일   초판 1쇄 발행 2012년 3월 12일

발행인 박효상   책임 편집 강성실   편집·진행 모희진 · 이종만   영업 이종선 · 이태호 · 이전희
기획 이희경   디자인 장선숙   삽화 오희정

출판등록 제 10-1835호   발행처 사람in   주소 121-839 서울시 마포구 서교동 378-16 4F
전화 02)338-3555(代)   팩스 02)338-3545(代)   E-mail saramin@netsgo.com   Homepage www.saramin.com

※ 책값은 뒤표지에 있습니다.   ※ 파본은 바꾸어 드립니다.

ⓒ Saramin 2012

ISBN 978-89-6049-293-6 18740   978-89-6049-211-0(set)

The Flying Trunk

written by H. C. Andersen   rewritten by Chalice Kerr   illustrated by Heejeong Oh   narrated by Nicole Dawson

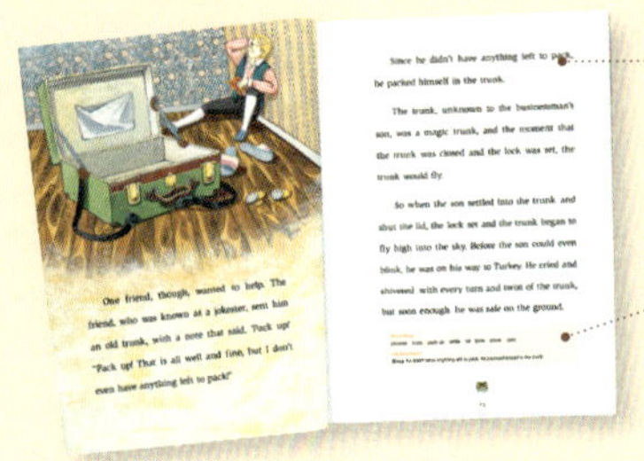

Story

본문에 표기되어 있는 끊어 읽기(✔)와 강세(●) 표시를 보면서
오디오를 듣고 스토리텔링해보세요.

Word Study & Key Expression

이야기를 이해하는 데 필수적으로 알아야 할 핵심 어휘와
표현입니다. 어휘와 표현의 해석과 해설은 사람in 홈페이지에서
보충학습 자료로 별도로 제공됩니다.

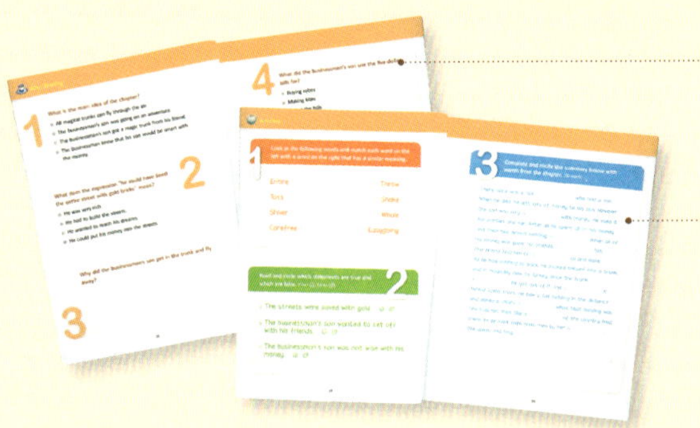

After Reading

각 챕터를 읽고 난 후 퀴즈를 통해
이해력을 측정해 봅니다.

Activities

각 챕터의 내용을 바탕으로
Matching, True or False,
Summary 등의 활동을 해봅니다.

Reading Diary

이야기를 모두 읽고 난 후 느낀 점과 이야기에 대한
자신의 생각을 간단히 정리해봄으로써
독서 감상문의 뼈대를 만들어봅니다.

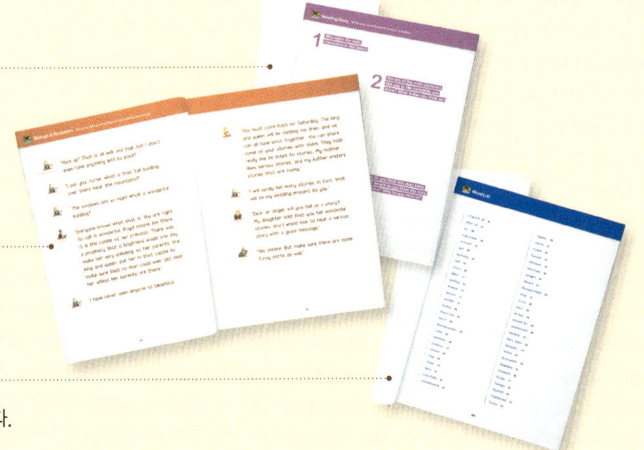

Dialogs & Recitation

스토리에 나온 대화문만을 모아 역할극(Role Play)에
활용해봅니다.

Word List

책에 나온 필수 어휘들을 알파벳순으로 정리하였습니다.

Audio 자료

Storytelling과 Read Along 두 가
지 버전의 MP3 파일이 제공되며
Word Study & Key Expression의
음원도 별도로 제공됩니다.

www. saramin. com

보충학습자료

스토리 본문, 어휘, Activities의 해석 및 해설
이 담겨 있는 보충학습자료를 사람in 홈페이
지(www.saramin.com)에서 PDF 파일로 다
운로드 받으실 수 있습니다.

Contents

The Flying Trunk

There once was a businessman who was smart in his business and became wealthy. When he died, he left a lot of money to his son. But the son was so careless with his money that he quickly used it all up. When his money was gone, most of his friends left him. One friend, though, sent him an old trunk. When he settled into the trunk, it began to fly high into the sky! Once it landed on its way to Turkey, he set off towards town and saw a tall castle near the mountains where the princess of the country lived. His new story started when he met the princess at the castle.

I like most when a nice man tells me stories.
I really love to listen to funny stories.
A good story should be serious and have a good message.
I have never met anyone as beautiful as her in the whole world!

The Magic Trunk

Once upon a time, there was a businessman who was quite wealthy. He was so rich that he could have lined the entire street with gold bricks, and he still would have had gold bricks left over. He would not waste his money like that though.

He was very smart in his business. He saved his money and made good choices. For every five cents that he spent, he earned a dollar.

When he died, he left a lot of money to his son. This made his son a very rich man. His son was not very smart though. He was a very carefree person and used the money to dress very finely and colorfully. He went to parties every evening.

He made kites out of five-dollar bills and flew them in the park. Instead of tossing stones in the river, he threw coins into the water. Because he was so careless with his money, he was soon left with almost nothing.

When he looked around his home, all he had left were a pair of slippers, an old robe, and four small coins. He did not know what to do. His friends were of no help. They deserted him when all his money was gone.

businessman   wealthy   line   choice   earn   carefree   dress   finely   colorfully
toss   careless   slippers   robe   desert

Key Expression

He was so rich that he **could have lined** the entire street with gold bricks, and he still **would have had** gold bricks left over.

One friend, though, wanted to help. The friend, who was known as a jokester, sent him an old trunk, with a note that said, 'Pack up!'

"Pack up! That is all well and fine, but I don't even have anything left to pack!"

Since he didn't have anything left to pack, he packed himself in the trunk.

The trunk, unknown to the businessman's son, was a magic trunk, and the moment that the trunk was closed and the lock was set, the trunk would fly.

So when the son settled into the trunk and shut the lid, the lock set and the trunk began to fly high into the sky. Before the son could even blink, he was on his way to Turkey. He cried and shivered with every turn and twist of the trunk, but soon enough he was safe on the ground.

jokester   trunk   pack up   settle   lid   blink   shiver   twist

Key Expression

Since he didn't have anything left to pack, he packed himself in the trunk.

Once the trunk landed, the businessman's son slowly opened the lid of the trunk and looked around. Seeing nobody around, he pushed the trunk out of the way and hid it behind some trees. Then, he set off for town.

When he got to town, the first person he met was a young child who was walking about with his nurse.

"I ask you, nurse, what is that tall building over there near the mountains?" the businessman's son asked. "The windows are so high! What a wonderful building!"

The nurse answered him, "Everyone knows

what that is. You are right to call it wonderful.

Royal people live there. It is the castle of our

princess. There was a prophecy that a boyfriend

would one day make her very unhappy. So her

parents, the king and queen, put her in that

castle to make sure that

no man could ever get

near her unless

her parents are

there."

1

What is the main idea of the chapter?

ⓐ All magical trunks can fly through the air.

ⓑ The businessman's son was going on an adventure.

ⓒ The businessman's son got a magic trunk from his friend.

ⓓ The businessman knew that his son would be smart with the money.

2

What does the expression "he could have lined the entire street with gold bricks" mean?

ⓐ He was very rich.

ⓑ He had to build the streets.

ⓒ He wanted to reach his dreams.

ⓓ He could put his money into the streets.

3

Why did the businessman's son get in the trunk and fly away?

What did the businessman's son use the five-dollar bills for?

  ⓐ Buying robes

  ⓑ Making kites

  ⓒ Paying the bills

  ⓓ Throwing parties

How did the businessman's son get to Turkey?

  ⓐ He walked there.

  ⓑ He flew in a plane.

  ⓒ He flew in a magical trunk.

  ⓓ He was sent there by a magic wand.

Why did probably the businessman's son hide the trunk behind some trees?

 **Activities**

1 Look at the following words and match each word on the left with a word on the right that has a similar meaning.

Entire •   • Throw

Toss •   • Shake

Shiver •   • Whole

Carefree •   • Easygoing

2 Read and circle which statements are true and which are false. (True= ☺, False= ☹)

ⓐ The streets were paved with gold. ☺ ☹

ⓑ The businessman's son wanted to set off with his friends. ☺ ☹

ⓒ The businessman's son was not wise with his money. ☺ ☹

There once was a rich ① ______________ who had a son.
When he died, he left lots of money to his son. However,
the son was very ② ______________ with money. He used it
for parties and fun. After all he spent all of his money
and then had almost nothing ③ ______________. When all of
his money was gone, his friends ④ ______________ him.
One friend sent him an old trunk, telling him to
⑤ ______________ up. As he had nothing to pack, he packed
himself into the trunk, and it magically flew to Turkey. Once
the trunk ⑥ ______________, he got out of it and
⑦ ______________ it behind some trees. He saw a tall building
in the distance and asked a child's ⑧ ______________ what
that building was. She told him that the ⑨ ______________ of
the country lived there to be kept safe from men by her
⑩ ______________, the queen and king.

Chapter 2

The Turkish Angel

The businessman's son thanked the nurse. He went back to the woods and dragged out his flying trunk. He stepped right into the trunk and flew up to the roof of the castle. As quietly as a mouse, he sneaked into the window of the castle.

It happened that the room he sneaked into was the princess's room. He saw the princess lying across the sofa and thought, 'I have never seen anyone so beautiful.' She looked so beautiful to him that he could not help but lean down and kiss her.

When the princess awoke, she was very frightened to see a strange man in her room, but he quickly told her that he was a Turkish angel sent to watch over her.

This made her feel much better. He sat down next to her and began to tell her fantastic stories. He told her fairy tales that delighted her, and he complimented her so nicely. When he asked her to marry him, she happily said yes.

"You must come back on Saturday. The king and queen will be visiting me then, and we can all have lunch together. You can share some of your stories with them. They both really like to listen to stories. My mother likes serious stories, and my father prefers stories that are funny."

"I will surely tell many stories. In fact, that will be my wedding present to you."

The son then went back out the window, got back into his trunk, and flew down to his hiding place. He placed the trunk back behind the trees where it would be hidden. He went back into town and bought himself a new suit. He wanted to look his best when he met the king and queen. He spent the rest of his time thinking of the perfect story to tell the royal couple.

When Saturday arrived, the businessman's son flew back to the castle and went inside. There, the princess introduced her love to her parents. The king and queen were quite happy to meet this handsome Turkish angel who wanted to marry their daughter.

They all had a lovely lunch, and then the queen asked, "Dear sir angel, will you tell us a story? My daughter said that you tell wonderful stories, and I would love to hear a serious story with a good message."

"Yes, please," said the king, "But make sure there are some funny parts as well."

"Of course, if a story would make your highnesses happy, I will tell you one."

1

What is the main idea of the chapter?

ⓐ The princess knew that she would have a visitor.

ⓑ The princess wanted to marry a handsome gentleman.

ⓒ The businessman's son tried to please the royal family.

ⓓ The king and queen have waited for someone to amuse them.

2

Which of the following did NOT the businessman's son do the first day he met the princess?

ⓐ He kissed her.

ⓑ He gave her a present.

ⓒ He complimented her.

ⓓ He asked her to marry him.

3

Why did the businessman's son decide to give stories to the princess as his wedding gift?

4 **When the businessman's son left the princess, he went into town to buy _______________.**

ⓐ a meal

ⓑ a new suit

ⓒ a place to live

ⓓ a wedding gift

What did the king asked the businessman's son?

ⓐ To make sure his story had a good message

ⓑ To make sure his story had some funny parts

ⓒ To make sure his story had an unexpected idea

ⓓ To make sure his story had some unique characters

6 **Why did probably the businessman's son spend time thinking of the perfect story to tell the royal couple?**

1

Look at the following words and match each with a word that means the opposite.

Delight •   • Funny

Serious •   • Partial

Perfect •   • Offend

Quietly •   • Loudly

2

Read and circle which statements are true and which are false. (True= , False=)

ⓐ The businessman's son came back on Saturday.

ⓑ The princess did not tell her parents about her love.

ⓒ The businessman's son left the castle through the gate.

Read the two summaries and decide which is better for this chapter. Then recite the summary.

ⓐ

The businessman's son flew up to the castle and sneaked into the princess's room. When the princess awoke, he told her he was a Turkish angel. He told her the most wonderful stories and asked her to marry him. She agreed, but asked him to tell her parents a story when he came back to the castle.

ⓑ

The businessman's son flew up to the castle, and met the princess. They decided to get married. First, though, the man had to get her parents' consent. So, he prepared a fantastic lunch for them when he came back to the castle. After lunch, the queen asked him to tell them a brilliant story to please both of her and her husband.

Chapter 3

The Story of the Household Items

He began at once with the perfect story.

"Once upon a time, there was a bunch of matches. Those matches were very proud of themselves. They came from no lowly shrubs but from the mightiest pine tree. This pine tree from which the matches came was the king of the forest. Now the matches found themselves lying on a kitchen counter in between the stove and an old copper pot. Their lives now were humble, but they remembered the past.

The matches said, 'Remember when we lived mightily in the forest? We were as free as birds, swaying in the wind as a giant pine tree. Our leaves were green and moved in the breeze.

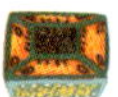

We felt the touch of the rain and the warmth of the sun. We were very rich indeed. Then came that terrible day when the woodcutter arrived as he tramped through the forest like a great herd of elephants. First, he made a great ship that would sail around the world, then he made chairs, tables, and couches, and, lastly, he made us, small, silly little matches. Once so great, now all we do is strike up a little light, a small spark.'

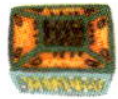

Word Study

sorrow   clean   serve   in service   trash   liquid   yard   share

Key Expression

The only time I have some happiness **is when** the family cleans me after dinner and
I sit outside in the yard to dry.

The copper pot listened to this tale of sorrow. She responded by saying, 'My story is a little different. My whole life has been about cleaning and serving. Ever since I was first made, I have been in service.

Whenever the family needs something to hold water, something to cook in, or something to hold trash, liquid, or food, they call upon me. The only time I have some happiness is when the family cleans me after dinner and I sit outside in the yard to dry. I am able to talk with my friends from this house. The market basket gives us all sorts of news from the market, and we share what we know with one another.

One day, the wooden bowl was so surprised by something he heard that he fell down and shattered right on the spot!'

'You talk too much,' said the matches, bumping against each other until sparks flew out from their bundle. 'We want to have a happy

evening. Let us talk about something more pleasant. We could talk about those of us who came from greatness, like us.'

The saucepan answered, 'I agree we should talk about something more interesting, but instead of talking about what we used to be, let's talk about something we've done or seen. That will be more interesting. One day, when I was much younger, I sat by the shore of the Baltic Sea, on the Danish shore.'

The plates cried out, 'Oh, what a wonderful way to begin a story. I am sure that it will be a wonderful tale!' 'When I was young,' continued the saucepan, 'I lived in a very quiet and calm family. The floors were cleaned every day, the sheets were washed every week, and the entire house was aired out every month. It was a very satisfactory life.'

The water bucket shouted out, 'Oh, what a beautiful way of telling a story you have! I can tell you came from a great family. There is a pure way about your stories.' The water bucket jumped around in excitement and spilled some water on the floor.

'Yes, well, thank you. As I was saying, life was very good.' The saucepan continued with his story, and it ended just as beautifully as it began. The plates clinked together with pleasure, and the broom brought out some green leaves to crown the saucepan king of the evening.

He hoped that, the next evening, the saucepan would crown him in return.

The fireplace poker jumped up from his place and cried out, 'Let's dance now!'

He danced across the floor and twirled around with such energy that the chair cushion in the corner began laughing. 'Will I be crowned king now?' asked the fireplace poker. The broom then found another crown of leaves and placed it on top of the fireplace poker.

Meanwhile, the matches were quite unhappy. 'They are just common people, after all,' the matches sniffed. The group asked the tea kettle to sing for them, but she refused because she had no boiling water in her.

Word Study

twirl   place   after all   sniff   kettle   refuse   boiling

Key Expression

He danced across the floor and twirled around with **such** energy **that** the chair cushion in the corner began laughing.

The rest of the household items thought she was just acting too good for them since she would sing for important guests inside the house. On the windowsill, there sat an old ink pen, which was quite fine. The ink pen said, 'If the tea kettle will not sing, it is okay. There is a nightingale in a cage hanging from the balcony. She will sing very prettily for us.' Everyone agreed that it would be a good plan to have the nightingale sing for them.

Everyone agreed, that is, except for the tea kettle. 'It is most inappropriate to have this strange, foreign bird sing for us! It is very unpatriotic. I bet the market basket could settle this argument for us.'

Word Study
household   windowsill   nightingale   balcony   except for   inappropriate   foreign
unpatriotic   bet   settle   argument

Key Expression
It is most inappropriate *to have* this strange, foreign bird sing for us!

The market basket did indeed settle things for them. 'I find all of this to be quite terrible. What a way to spend an evening! We could have been putting the house into some sort of order, but, instead, we sat around telling stories. If we put the house in order, then I could lead a game afterwards, and we would all be happy. We could act out a play,' shouted the market basket just as the door opened. A serving girl walked into the room.

Everyone stayed very still; even though they had fun together, they were all very proud and knew that if they were in charge, they would make the best decisions.

The serving girl grabbed the matches and lit one. The room blazed in a glory of light.

The matches thought, 'Now everyone will see that we are the best, for we are the ones the serving girl reached for first.'

Just as that thought was finished, the matches flickered and burned out."

1

What is the main idea of the chapter?

ⓐ Each of the household items had their own story.

ⓑ The matches were arrogant and full of complaints.

ⓒ The water bucket was influenced by others too easily.

ⓓ The saucepan was did not care how others felt about him.

2

Whose story is most favored by the household items?

ⓐ The matches

ⓑ The tea kettle

ⓒ The copper pot

ⓓ The saucepan

3

The only time the copper pot have some happiness is when ________________________.

4   Every household item stayed still when

___________________.

ⓐ the copper pot shouted

ⓑ the matches burned out

ⓒ the serving girl walked into the room

ⓓ the market basket settled their argument

The matches thought they were better than everyone else because __________________________.

ⓐ they could make fire

ⓑ everybody liked their story

ⓒ the serving girl reached for them first

ⓓ they looked better than the others

Why did the tea kettle NOT want the nightingale to sing for them?

1

Look at the following words and match each word on the left with a word on the right that has a similar meaning.

Bump •   • Poor

Humble •   • Rock

Mighty •   • Hit

Sway •   • Powerful

2

Read and circle which statements are true and which are false. (True= 🙂, False= 🙁)

ⓐ The matches were happy with their situation.   🙂 🙁

ⓑ The first item the woodcutter made was chairs.   🙂 🙁

ⓒ The market basket knew all of news from the market.   🙂 🙁

ⓓ The fireplace poker suggested all the household items to dance.   🙂 🙁

Complete and recite the summary below with words from the chapter. (10 words)

The businessman's son made his story about the

① ______________ items: The matches are very proud of

themselves because they came from the ② ______________

pine trees. The copper pot says that her story is

different. Her whole life has been about ③ ______________

and serving. The matches want to talk about something

more pleasant and the ④ ______________ agree. When his

story ends beautifully, the broom brings out some green

leaves to ⑤ ______________ him king of the evening. The

⑥ ______________ poker dances across the floor in

excitement. The group ask the tea ⑦ ______________ to

sing for them, but she refuses. When there is an

⑧ ______________ about who to sing, the market basket

settles it. Soon after, a serving girl walks into the room

and ⑨ ______________ the matches. Then, the matches

⑩ ______________ and burn out, feeling proud.

Chapter 4

The Angel Flies Away

As the businessman's son finished the story, the queen clapped her hands together and laughed. "What a fantastic story," she exclaimed. "I felt like I was really there in the kitchen talking with the matches. Of course, you shall have our daughter's hand in marriage."

"Yes, son, welcome to our family. Our daughter shall be lucky to have you."

They set a date for the wedding, and the evening before the wedding, the entire city was lit up, just like the kitchen in the story was lit up by matches. Cakes and candies were passed out to everyone in the streets.

Boys ran throughout, yelling "Hurray! Hurray!"

Word Study

clap   exclaim   marriage   entire   pass out   throughout   hurray

Key Expression

Of course, you **shall** have our daughter's hand in marriage.

The businessman's son was so happy that he decided to give the people another surprise. He bought many firecrackers and fireworks and passed them out to everyone he saw. Soon, the skies were lit up with bright bursts of color, and sparks were flying everywhere. The people had never seen such a sight!

They truly believed, after this, that their princess was marrying a Turkish angel. The son now got into his trunk and flew around, watching the faces of the people as they saw the beautiful fireworks.

He finally set down the flying trunk and began talking to the people. Everyone he talked

to had something nice to say, and, at the end of the night, the man was quite pleased. Knowing that he was to be married the next morning, he ran back to his flying trunk and decided to go back to the castle.

Though he looked everywhere, his trunk was nowhere to be found. It had been burned to ashes in the fireworks. Since the trunk was missing, the businessman's son could not fly anywhere. He could not, in fact, fly to his own wedding.

The princess waited all day. She stood out on her balcony and looked for her Turkish angel, but he never came. She still waits today, the stories say, disappointed by her love, just as was foretold.

The businessman's son is still wandering the earth, walking from town to town and telling stories, but none of them is as good as his story about the matches.

1

What is the main idea of the chapter?

ⓐ Fireworks are dangerous.

ⓑ The businessman's son caused a great many fires.

ⓒ The prophecy about the princess did not come true.

ⓓ The businessman's son lost his trunk and missed his own wedding.

2

What does the expression "the people had never seen such a sight" mean?

ⓐ They were scared.

ⓑ They did not love it.

ⓒ They had never witnessed anything like that before.

ⓓ They were too busy to take time to look up the sky.

3

Why could the businessman's son NOT find his flying trunk?

When did the people believe that their princess was marrying a Turkish angel?

ⓐ After the fireworks

ⓑ Before the fireworks

ⓒ On the day of the wedding

ⓓ When they saw the flying trunk

Where did the princess wait for the businessman's son?

ⓐ By the trees

ⓑ On her balcony

ⓒ In her courtyard

ⓓ In the wedding chapel

Why could the businessman's son NOT go to his wedding?

1 Look at the following words and match each with a word that means the opposite.

Finish •　　　　　　　• Start

Pleased •　　　　　　　• Unhappy

Missing •　　　　　　　• Satisfied

Disappointed •　　　　　　• Found

2 Read and circle which statements are true and which are false. (True= ☺, False= ☹)

ⓐ The king burned the flying trunk.　☺ ☹

ⓑ Everyone in the streets received cakes and candies.　☺ ☹

ⓒ The princess did not wait for the businessman's son.　☺ ☹

ⓓ The businessman's son wandered the earth endlessly and told stories.　☺ ☹

Read the two summaries and decide which is better for this chapter. Then recite the summary.

ⓐ

The king and queen both liked the businessman's son's story. They agreed that he should marry their daughter. The day before the wedding, the businessman's son bought fireworks for the people of the city and flew around in his trunk, watching all of the people. He then landed on the ground and talked to the people. When he ran back to his flying trunk, it had been burned up by the fireworks. As he could not fly, he could not go to his own wedding.

ⓑ

The queen liked the businessman's son's story, but the king found it boring. They were forced to allow him to marry their daughter because the princess insisted. The businessman's son passed out fireworks to the people of the city. While he watched the beautiful fireworks with them, someone stole the flying trunk. As a result, the princess was left sad all of her days, and the businessman's son is still wandering all over the earth.

Chapter 1 After Reading p.16

1 ⓒ

2 ⓐ

3 His friend advised him to pack up and leave, but he had nothing to pack up. So he got inside the trunk, and it started to fly when he closed it.

4 ⓑ

5 ⓒ

6 He probably hid the trunk so that nobody would discover his secret. Maybe he did not want anyone to steal it either.

Chapter 1 Activity p.18

1 Entire - Whole
Toss - Throw
Shiver - Shake
Carefree - Easygoing

2 ⓐ ☹
   ⓑ ☹
   ⓒ ☺

3 ① businessman ② careless
   ③ left   ④ deserted
   ⑤ pack   ⑥ landed
   ⑦ hid   ⑧ nurse
   ⑨ princess   ⑩ parents

Chapter 2 After Reading p.28

1 ⓒ

2 ⓑ

3 Because she loved his stories and he felt that her parents would love them also.

4 ⓑ

5 ⓑ

6 He probably wanted to please the royal couple so that he could make them allow him to marry the princess.

Chapter 2 Activity p.30

1 Delight - Offend
Serious - Funny
Perfect - Partial
Quietly - Loudly

2 ⓐ ☺
   ⓑ ☹
   ⓒ ☹

3 ⓐ

1 ⓐ

2 ⓓ

3 the family cleans her after dinner and she sits outside in the yard to dry.

4 ⓒ

5 ⓒ

6 The tea kettle thought it would be unpatriotic since the nightingale was a foreign bird.

Chapter 3 Activity p.50

1 Bump - Hit
Humble - Poor
Mighty - Powerful
Sway - Rock

2 ⓐ ☹
ⓑ ☹
ⓒ ☺
ⓓ ☺

3 ① household   ② mightiest
③ cleaning   ④ saucepan
⑤ crown   ⑥ fireplace
⑦ kettle   ⑧ argument
⑨ lights   ⑩ flicker

Chapter 4 After Reading p.60

1 ⓓ

2 ⓒ

3 The trunk caught fire because of a spark from the fireworks, and it burned to ashes.

4 ⓐ

5 ⓑ

6 Since his flying trunk was missing, he could not fly anywhere.

Chapter 4 Activity p.62

1 Finish - Start
Pleased - Unhappy
Missing - Found
Disappointed - Satisfied

2 ⓐ ☹
ⓑ ☺
ⓒ ☹
ⓓ ☺

3 ⓐ

Reading Diary
Dialogs & Recitation

1 Who is/are the main character(s) in this story?

2 Are any of the main characters like you or like somebody you know? What makes you think so?

3 Describe your favorite character in this story and tell me why the character is your favorite.

4 When do you think this story takes place? Where do you think this story takes place? Why do you think so?

5 What is the funniest/scariest/best part of this story?

6 Is there a problem in this story?
If so, how does the problem get solved?
How would you have solved the problem?

7 Would any of your friends/family enjoy this story? Why or why not?

8 Could you come up with another good title for this story? What would it be?

9 If you could change the ending of this story, what would it be?

10 Do you think this story would make a good movie? Why or why not?

The businessman's son

"Pack up! That is all well and fine, but I don't even have anything left to pack!"

"I ask you, nurse, what is that tall building over there near the mountains?"

"The windows are so high! What a wonderful building!"

Nurse

"Everyone knows what that is. You are right to call it wonderful. Royal people live there. It is the castle of our princess. There was a prophecy that a boyfriend would one day make her very unhappy, so her parents, the king and queen, put her in that castle to make sure that no man could ever get near her unless her parents are there."

'I have never seen anyone so beautiful.'

Princess

"You must come back on Saturday. The king and queen will be visiting me then, and we can all have lunch together. You can share some of your stories with them. They both really like to listen to stories. My mother likes serious stories, and my father prefers stories that are funny."

"I will surely tell many stories. In fact, that will be my wedding present to you."

Queen

"Dear sir angel, will you tell us a story? My daughter said that you tell wonderful stories, and I would love to hear a serious story with a good message."

King

"Yes, please. But make sure there are some funny parts as well."

Matches

"Remember when we lived mightily in the forest? We were as free as birds, swaying in the wind as a giant pine tree. Our leaves were green and moved in the breeze. We felt the touch of the rain and the warmth of the sun. We were very rich indeed."

Then came that terrible day when the woodcutter arrived as he tramped through the forest like a great herd of elephants. First, he made a great ship that would sail around the world, then he made chairs, tables, and couches, and, lastly, he made us, small, silly little matches. Once so great, now all we do is strike up a little light, a small spark.

Copper pot

"My story is a little different. My whole life has been about cleaning and serving. Ever since I was first made, I have been in service. Whenever the family needs something to hold water, something to cook in, or something to hold trash, liquid, or food, they call upon me. The only time I have some happiness is when the family cleans me after dinner and I sit outside in the yard to dry. I am able to talk with my friends from this house. The market basket gives us all sorts of news from the market, and we share what we know with one another."

"You talk too much."

"We want to have a happy evening. Let us talk about something more pleasant. We could talk about those of us who came from greatness, like us."

Saucepan

"I agree we should talk about something more interesting, but instead of talking about what we used to be, let's talk about something we've done or seen. That will be more interesting. One day, when I was much younger, I sat by the shore of the Baltic Sea, on the Danish shore."

Plates

"Oh, what a wonderful way to begin a story. I am sure that it will be a wonderful tale!"

"When I was young, I lived in a very quiet and calm family. The floors were cleaned every day, the sheets were washed every week, and the entire house was aired out every month. It was a very satisfactory life."

Water Bucket

"Oh, what a beautiful way of telling a story you have! I can tell you came from a great family. There is a pure way about your stories."

"Yes, well, thank you. As I was saying, life was very good."

"Let's dance now!"

Fireplace poker

"Will I be crowned king now?"

"They are just common people, after all."

"If the tea kettle will not sing, it is okay. There is a nightingale in a cage hanging from the balcony. He will sing very prettily for us."

Ink pen

Tea Kettle

"It is most inappropriate to have this strange, foreign bird sing for us! It is very unpatriotic. I bet the market basket could settle this argument for us."

Market Basket

"I find all of this to be quite terrible. What a way to spend an evening! We could have been putting the house into some sort of order, but, instead, we sat around telling stories. If we put the house in order, then I could lead a game afterwards, and we would all be happy. We could act out a play."

"Now everyone will see that we are the best, for we are the ones the serving girl reached for first."

"What a fantastic story."

"I felt like I was really there in the kitchen talking with the matches. Of course, you shall have our daughter's hand in marriage."

"Yes, son, welcome to our family. Our daughter shall be lucky to have you."

Boys

"Hurray! Hurray!"